SUPER CUTE!

Baby Cats

by Bethany Olson

BELLWETHER MEDIA • MINNEAPOLIS, MN

Note to Librarians, Teachers, and Parents:

Blastoff! Readers are carefully developed by literacy experts and combine standards-based content with developmentally appropriate text.

Level 1 provides the most support through repetition of high-frequency words, light text, predictable sentence patterns, and strong visual support.

Level 2 offers early readers a bit more challenge through varied simple sentences, increased text load, and less repetition of high-frequency words.

Level 3 advances early-fluent readers toward fluency through increased text and concept load, less reliance on visuals, longer sentences, and more literary language.

Level 4 builds reading stamina by providing more text per page, increased use of punctuation, greater variation in sentence patterns, and increasingly challenging vocabulary.

Level 5 encourages children to move from "learning to read" to "reading to learn" by providing even more text, varied writing styles, and less familiar topics.

Whichever book is right for your reader, Blastoff! Readers are the perfect books to build confidence and encourage a love of reading that will last a lifetime!

This edition first published in 2014 by Bellwether Media, Inc.

No part of this publication may be reproduced in whole or in part without written permission of the publisher. For information regarding permission, write to Bellwether Media, Inc., Attention: Permissions Department, 5357 Penn Avenue South, Minneapolis, MN 55419.

Library of Congress Cataloging-in-Publication Data

Olson, Bethany.
 Baby cats / by Bethany Olson.
   p. cm. – (Blastoff readers. Super cute!)
 Audience: K to grade 3.
 Summary: "Developed by literacy experts for students in kindergarten through grade three, this book introduces baby cats to young readers through leveled text and related photos"– Provided by publisher.
 Includes bibliographical references and index.
 ISBN 978-1-60014-923-8 (hardcover : alk. paper)
 1. Kittens–Juvenile literature. 2. Cats–Juvenile literature. 3. Animals–Infancy–Juvenile literature. I. Title.
 SF445.7.O47 2014
 636.807–dc23
                                                                    2013009635

Text copyright © 2014 by Bellwether Media, Inc. BLASTOFF! READERS and associated logos are trademarks and/or registered trademarks of Bellwether Media, Inc. SCHOLASTIC, CHILDREN'S PRESS, and associated logos are trademarks and/or registered trademarks of Scholastic Inc.

Printed in the United States of America, North Mankato, MN.

Table of Contents

Kittens!

Kittens are
baby cats.
They are often
born in a **litter**
of three to five.

Brothers and
sisters cuddle
close to
stay warm.

Life With Mom

Little kittens also snuggle with mom. Her fur makes a soft blanket.

Sometimes mom carries her kittens. She picks them up with her teeth.

The kittens cry when they are hungry. They **purr** as they drink mom's milk.

They also purr when mom **grooms** them.

Growing Kittens

Older kittens groom themselves. They lick their paws and wipe their faces.

Kittens **pounce** on top of one another. This is how they play.

Then kittens stretch
out to relax.
Big yawn!

Glossary

grooms–cleans

litter–a group of babies born together

pounce–to jump on suddenly

purr–to make a low, soft hum

To Learn More

AT THE LIBRARY

Corse, Nicole. *Puppies and Kittens*. New York, N.Y.: Scholastic, 2010.

DK Publishing. *Touch and Feel: Kitten*. New York, N.Y.: DK Publishing, 2011.

Elora, Grace. *Kittens*. New York, N.Y.: Gareth Stevens Pub., 2011.

ON THE WEB

Learning more about cats is as easy as 1, 2, 3.

1. Go to www.factsurfer.com.

2. Enter "cats" into the search box.

3. Click the "Surf" button and you will see a list of related Web sites.

With factsurfer.com, finding more information is just a click away.

Index

The images in this book are reproduced through the courtesy of: Dmitry Kalinovsky, front cover;
Kristian Sekulic, pp. 4-5; Juniors/ SuperStock, pp. 6-7; John Daniels/ Ardea, pp. 8-9; Labat-Rouquette/
Kimball Stock, pp. 10-11; Digidreamgrafix, pp. 12-13; Biosphoto/ SuperStock, pp. 14-15; Juniors/
Glow Images, pp. 16-17; Age Fotostock/ SuperStock, pp. 18-19; Oksun70, pp. 20-21.